DATE DUE			

615014 01695   21866C   045

GROWING
TREES

Tracy Nelson Maurer

The Rourke Book Company, Inc.
Vero Beach, Florida 32964

Tracy Nelson Maurer specializes in nonfiction and business writing. Her most recently published children's books include the Bodyworks series, also from Rourke Publishing. A graduate of the University of Minnesota Journalism School, Tracy lives with her husband Mike and two children in Superior, Wisconsin.

With appreciation to gardeners Lois M. Nelson, Harvey Almstedt, and Lois I. Nelson; and to Richard J. Zondag, Jung Seed Company.

PHOTO CREDITS:
All photos and illustrations © East Coast Studios except p. 18, © T. Maurer; and p. 21, © David and Patricia Armentrout

PRODUCED & DESIGNED by East Coast Studios
eastcoaststudios.com

EDITORIAL SERVICES:
Lois M. Nelson
Pamela Schroeder

Library of Congress Cataloging-in-Publication Data

Maurer, Tracy, 1965-
    Growing trees / Tracy Nelson Maurer.
        p. cm. — (Green thumb guides)
    Includes bibliographical references (p.).
    Summary: Describes how to plant, care for, prune, and protect various kinds of trees.
    ISBN 1-55916-255-4
    1. Trees—Juvenile literature. 2. Trees, Care of—Juvenile literature. [1. Trees.] I. Title.

SB435 .M38 2000
635.9'77—dc21

                                                                00–026340

Printed in the USA

Table of Contents

Tall Trees, Small Trees 5

Woody Plants..................................6

Room to Grow.................................8

Sun and Wind 11

Planting Trees................................12

Feed the Trees 14

Time for a Trim 17

Pests...18

Special Trees to Grow.......................20

Glossary 23

Index...24

Further Reading..............................24

Tall Trees, Small Trees

Tall trees line city streets and country roads. People plant trees for shade and to stop wind. Trees add color and shape to yards and parks. Kids climb trees and build forts in them, too!

Like trees, shrubs make yards look pretty. People often plant a line of shrubs, called a hedge, between yards. Thorny shrubs next to a house help keep prowlers away.

Both trees and shrubs help clean the air. They breathe in old air and send out fresh air.

Fun Fact
Aspirin comes from the bark of the willow tree. People also make syrup, rubber, lumber, paper, fabric, and fuel from trees.

Animals and birds live in many of the trees people plant. Kids also like to play in trees!

Woody Plants

Trees and shrubs, or woody plants, come in very different shapes and sizes. However, all woody plants do one amazing thing. Their woody stems, or trunks, live through winter year after year. A Douglas fir tree can live more than 1,000 years!

The leaves of deciduous trees turn colors in the fall. The stems, or trunks, stay alive—even through cold winters.

Evergreens have green leaves, or needles, in every season.

Gardeners must choose to plant **deciduous** (di SIJ oo us) trees or **evergreens** (EV ur greenz). Some people call deciduous trees broadleafs. These trees grow leaves that turn colors in the fall. Evergreens, also called pine trees or **conifers** (KON uh firz), grow skinny needles and look green all year.

Fun Fact

One evergreen does not stay green all year. The tamarack, or larch, turns yellow in the fall and loses its needles.

Room to Grow

Trees grow very slowly. You might be a grandparent when your trees reach only half of their full size! Before you plant trees or shrubs, it's important to know how big they will grow. Be sure to plant away from power lines or buildings.

Shrubs usually grow faster than trees. Some shrubs, such as lilacs, grow more stems every year. They get very large. Plant your new shrubs with enough space to grow.

Fun Fact
How old is a tree? If it is cut down already, count the rings inside the tree trunk. Each ring equals about a year.

These trees grew under power lines. The electric company prunes the trees for safety.

Sun and Wind

Woody plants need sunlight, air, water, and soil to grow. Different kinds of trees and shrubs live and grow in different places.

Think about where your plants will grow best. Deciduous plants like places with more sunshine than evergreens do.

Many trees or shrubs need to keep away from winter winds. Winds dry out the needles or leaves. Some gardeners even wrap their shrubs in **burlap** (BUR lap) coats.

These shrubs like sunny and warm weather all year long. If you live where it snows in the winter, you can grow shrubs like these in pots. Move them indoors in the winter.

Planting Trees

Gardeners buy trees or shrubs from catalogs, nurseries, or garden centers. Some plants are in large pots. Others are bare-root, or without soil. You may also buy plants with the roots and soil, called the root ball, wrapped in burlap.

This nursery sells trees with the root balls wrapped in burlap.

Dig a hole deep enough so that the top of the root ball is even with the yard around it.

For most woody plants, you should dig a hole at least six inches larger than the root ball. Gently set the roots in the hole. Fill the hole with soil. Pat the soil down. Water your new plant right away.

Feed the Trees

Gardeners know that soil is important to healthy plants. It keeps the plant strong. Soil also holds food, water, and air. Roots work like underground branches to carry **nutrients** (NEW tree ents) from the soil to the stem, or trunk.

Woody plants drink about one inch of water each week. Gardeners often add special food, called **fertilizers** (FUR tuh LIE zurz), to make the soil better for the trees and shrubs.

Fun Fact
Some fertilizers change how plants look. Putting a special acid fertilizer around a hydrangea shrub turns its flowers from pink to blue!

Tree roots look like underground branches. Water the ground under your tree from the trunk out to the drip line. This helps bring water to all of the roots.

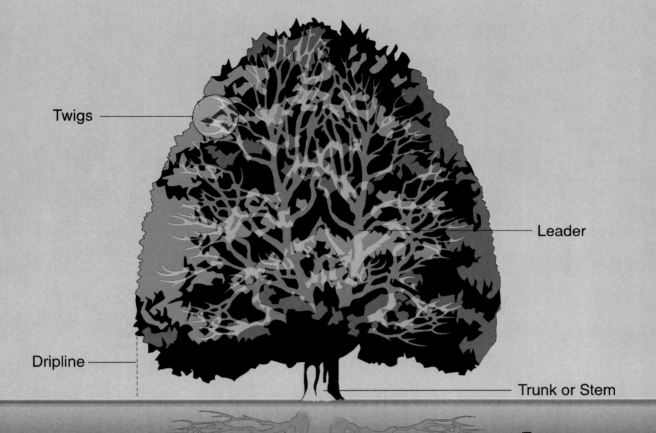
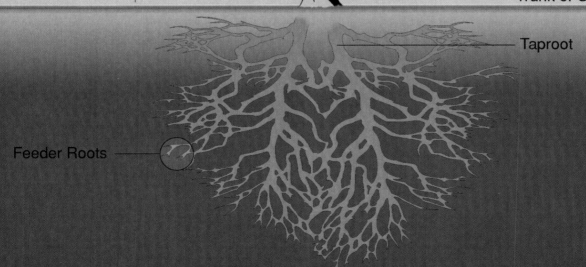

Twigs

Leader

Dripline

Trunk or Stem

Taproot

Feeder Roots

Time for a Trim

Most woody plants need little care. Pruning, or cutting branches, helps trees and shrubs get strong and grow more flowers and fruit. Always ask an adult to help prune trees or shrubs.

Gardeners "shear" or "thin" when they prune. Shearing looks like a shrub haircut. Every branch gets a little trimmed off. Thinning means cutting off a few lower branches to give the plant room to grow.

Sometimes gardeners prune shrubs to make fancy hedges or **topiaries** (TOE pee AIR eez). Animal shapes make fun topiary designs!

Fun Fact
Flat trees, or espaliers, work well in small yards. Careful pruning keeps these trees, shrubs, or vines growing flat along a fence.

The topiary in this picture looks like a green dinosaur.

Pests

People enjoy trees. Animals, birds, and insects also like trees, but for different reasons.

Rabbits, deer, and other hungry animals eat the tree bark. Bears climb trees for fruit or berries. They often break the branches. Woodpeckers poke deep holes into the bark when they hunt for insects. Those insects can hurt the tree, too.

The pipe on this apple tree protects the bark from rabbits and mice during the winter. It will come off in the spring when the tree begins to grow again.

Machines can hurt trees. Here, a trimmer has cut into the bark many times.

Trees can also be hurt by machines, such as lawnmowers, snowplows, and bulldozers.

Wrap the tree trunk in special tree tape or put up a small metal fence.

Special Trees to Grow

Many gardeners enjoy taking care of special trees or shrubs. Growing bonsai (BON zih) trees is an art form that began in Asia more than a 1,000 years ago. Bonsai artists prune roots and branches to keep these trees tiny.

Some gardeners grow **dwarf** (DWORF) trees that bear full-size fruits. They put a normal fruit tree top together with a dwarf tree bottom. These special trees are planted in pots to move inside for winter.

Other gardeners grow Christmas trees, maple-syrup trees, or only one kind of shrub, such as camellias. Grow what makes you happy!

Fun Fact
A Christmas tree takes about ten years to get big enough to cut.

Bonsai trees look like the wind has twisted and shaped them.

GLOSSARY

burlap (BUR lap) — a lightweight, scratchy fabric

conifers (KON uh firz) — trees or shrubs that have seeds in cones

deciduous (di SIJ oo us) — trees that shed their leaves in the fall

dwarf (DWORF) — in gardening, a fully grown plant that is much smaller than the usual size

evergreens (EV ur greenz) — trees or shrubs that have green leaves all year

fertilizers (FUR tuh LIE zurz) — nutrients for plants that gardeners add to the soil

nutrients (NEW tree ents) — food for energy to grow

topiaries (TOE pee AIR eez) — plants trimmed into fancy shapes or animals

Where winters stay warm, gardeners can grow grapefruit and orange trees outdoors.

INDEX

bonsai   20

burlap   11, 12

deciduous   7, 11

dwarf   20

evergreens   7, 11

fertilizers   14

hedge   5, 17

nutrients   14

prowlers   5

prune   17, 20

root ball   12, 13

soil   11, 12, 13, 14

topiary   17

woody plants   6, 11, 13, 14, 17

FURTHER READING

Find out more about gardening with these helpful books:

• Ambler, Wayne et al. *Treasury of Gardening.* Lincolnwood, Ill.: Publications International, 1994.

• Hart, Avery, and Paul Mantell. *Kids Garden!: The Anytime, Anyplace Guide To Sowing & Growing Fun.* Charlotte, Vermont: Williamson Publishing Co., 1996.

• *Rodale's Illustrated Encyclopedia of Gardening and Landscaping Techniques.* Edited by Barbara W. Ellis. Emmaus, Penn.: Rodale Press, 1990.

On-line resources:

Search for "kids gardening" on the World Wide Web to see many different sites.

• www.garden.org (c) National Gardening Association, 1999.

• www.bonsaiweb.com (c) BonsaiWeb 1999.